CLARITY IS POWER

Q & A

“Clarity is Power" book series, is a collection of wisdom from thought-provoking Q and A with renowned Mahatria. His unique gift of answering questions spontaneously is captured in this book, offering life-changing insights.

The "Clarity is Power" series comprises 11 illuminating volumes, each addressing essential aspects of life:

1. Attitudes
2. Self-Discipline
3. Emotional Development
4. Relationships
5. Marriage
6. Parenting
7. Student Life
8. Career Growth
9. Leadership and Entrepreneurship
10. Spirituality
11. Faith

Mahatria Spiritualist | Thought leader | Diviner of infinitheism

For nearly three decades, Mahatria has empowered millions worldwide to achieve holistic abundance. His profound wisdom uplifts people in health, wealth, love, bliss, and spirituality.

infinitheism, the path divined by Mahatria, inspires breakthroughs for anyone who ardently desires abundance by transforming the human spirit to have faith in its infinite potential.

First published in India

MANJUL

Manjul Publishing House

• 2nd Floor, Usha Preet Complex,
42 Malviya Nagar, Bhopal 462 003 - India
• C-16, Sector 3, Noida, Uttar Pradesh 201301 – India
Website: www.manjulindia.com

Distribution Centres:
Ahmedabad, Bengaluru, Bhopal, Kolkata, Chennai,
Hyderabad, Mumbai, New Delhi, Pune

In association with:

infinitheism

3, 3rd Cross Road, R A Puram,
Chennai, Tamil Nadu, India
www.infinitheism.com

SELF-DISCIPLINE (CLARITY IS POWER)

by

mahatria Ra

This edition first published in 2016
Third impression 2024

ISBN 978-93-5543-431-9

Printed and bound in India by Thomson Press (India) Ltd.

CLARITY IS POWER

Q&A

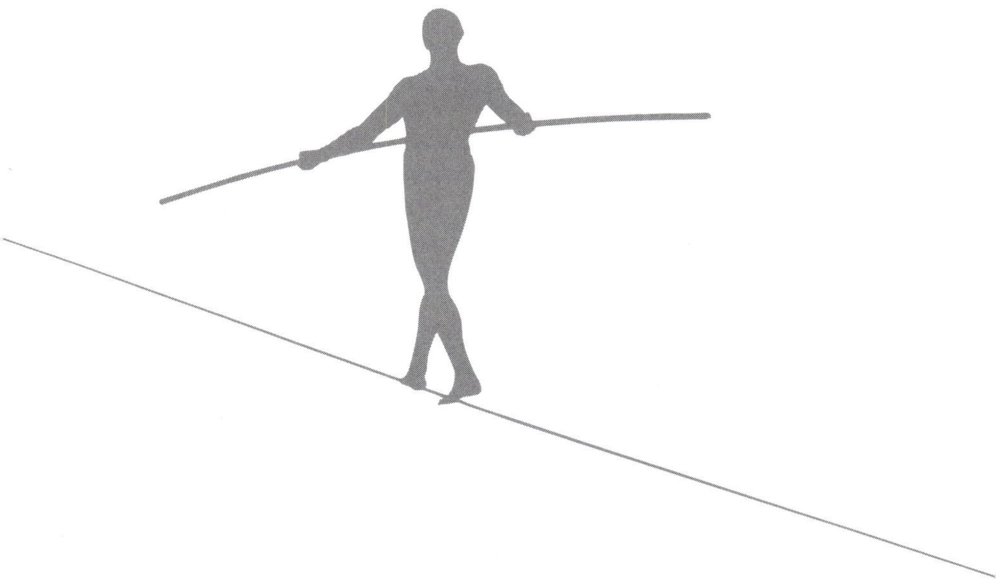

SELF-DISCIPLINE

mahātria

CONTENTS

CONTENTS

> *My negative and positive emotions are at war. It seems the positives lose to negatives. How can I make the positives win?*

To let the positive win over the negative, you must first understand the differences between positive and negative emotions.

When someone is doing something in a way I don't want it to be done, and I am not able to accept it, I become angry. However, even though someone is doing something in a way I don't want it to be done, I am able to accept it; I remain tolerant.

When someone has something which I don't have, and I am not able to accept it, I become jealous. However, even though someone has something which I don't have and I am able to accept it, I get inspired.

When someone has done something that has emotionally hurt me, and I am not able to accept it, it develops hatred in me. However, even though someone has done something that has emotionally hurt me, I am able to accept it; hence it helps me forgive them.

So, it is not 'something' or 'someone' that is making me feel positive or negative, but it is my 'acceptance' or 'non-acceptance' of that something or that someone, which is making me feel positive or negative. It isn't the world, but the quality of my response to the world (acceptance or non-acceptance) that determines the quality of my emotions.

Next time you feel disturbed with a negative emotion, instead of asking who or what is disturbing you, examine who or what you are resisting (not accepting) that is causing this disturbance in you. Replace resistance (non-acceptance) with acceptance, and the negative emotion will turn into a positive one.

Emotional management begins by stopping the blame game on 'something' or 'someone' and starting to take the responsibility to respond to life with 'acceptance'.

This exercise of awareness and introspection, when practiced long enough, will eventually enable the positive emotions to prevail over the negative emotions. A time can come in your life when the negative emotions will not even be born anymore.

❝

Emotional management begins by stopping blaming that 'something' or 'someone' and starting to take the responsibility to respond to life with 'acceptance'.

mahātria

2

Where is the time to
invest on the 48 things
in which I want to grow,
when I just have 24 hours?

To think there isn't enough time is madness. The fact is not that we don't have enough time, but our time is mindlessly being stolen by the 'trivial many', which has little or no consequences on the overall effectiveness of our life. There are too many time stealers in each of our lives. Identify your time stealers and stop giving them your time. Contrary to what time management gurus have taught us - that is to compile a 'To do list', we first need to prepare a 'Need not do list'.

A big 'no no' to mindless watching of mega-serials in television. A big 'no no' to 'at the door', then 'at the gate' and finally near the car park gossip. A big 'no no' to the compulsive habit of reading everything in a newspaper from obituaries to tender notices. A big 'no no' to becoming a member of every association and then attending those weekly meetings just because I have a social obligation to do so. A big 'no no' to late-night parties, for it does affect my efficiency the following morning. The list is endless...

Large parts of our days get wasted. A tragic amount of time gets wasted everywhere and by everybody. The starting point to revolutionise the way we use our time is to be honest with ourselves and confess that we are inefficient in the way we use our time.

The timeless wisdom is, "That on which you invest time, grows." If your business has been doing well, it is because you have been investing time on it. Even within business, if your Northern region is doing well, it is because you have been investing time on it. If your social circle is expanding, it is because you have been investing time on it.

If your family life is deteriorating, it is because you have not been investing time on your family. If any of your relationship is not what it used to be, it is because you have not been investing time on that relationship. If your health is deteriorating, it is because you have not been investing time on it. After all, the opposite is also true, "That which is starved of time, shrinks."

Enlist all the redundant roles of your life that is robbing you of your precious time and vouch not to give those redundant roles any of your time any more. You will free yourself of so much time by withdrawing from the 'trivial many' so that now you will have time for every important aspect of your life. The quality of your life depends on your ability to say 'Yes' to what is important, and more importantly, the discipline to say 'No' to the 'don't have to do' aspects of life.

There is lot more time than we can use, if we begin to use it wisely. Before giving your time to anything, ask yourself, "Is it worth my time?"

The timeless wisdom is,
"That on which
you invest time, grows."

mahātria

In the process of attaining
clarity in a particular subject,
the element of confusion
takes its role and spoils
the strength of clarity.
Questions - Answers
- Again questions...
Can you please guide me?

Questions always precede answers. Problems always precede solutions. Chaos always precedes clarity. But... You cannot find an answer with the same maturity with which you formed the question. You cannot solve a problem with the same maturity with which you encountered it. You cannot gain clarity in a subject with the same maturity with which the confusion was understood.

Either you have to gain a higher maturity through your own contemplation and experiences, from which you find the answer, the solution and the clarity required; or you will have to take the help of one with a higher maturity, who will give you the answer, solution and clarity, and thus lead you to a higher maturity.

Those like you, who rely on your own intelligence first before falling back on an external intelligence, cannot avoid the chaotic and confusing transition. The moment you feed your intelligence with a subject, it immediately starts wandering in all possible directions. It forms questions; it answers its own questions; and then again questions its own answers. It seeks information on the subject from every possible source - human, literature and technology. It attempts to correlate the bits and pieces it has gathered. It tries to connect the dots. This is what contemplation is all about. But in all this, through what you call confusion and chaos, the maturity with which you look at the subject is expanded. Now, the maturity with which you are attempting to clarify the confusion is much higher. Now, even if you don't find the answer, the intelligence with which you look at things is much higher. So often, contemplating on one subject, helps you to gain clarity in one of your earlier confusions; you find answers to one of your unanswered questions from the past. That's why a human being is called an evolving consciousness.

Don't approach contemplation with an academic bent of mind, where you need to always have the right answer for every question. Enjoy the confusion. Wonder at how you are able to think. See contemplation as an intellectual game. And this game is such, you may not always find the treasure you are looking for, but you will find something else that you will treasure.

“

***You cannot find an answer
with the same maturity
with which you formed the question.
You cannot solve a problem
with the same maturity
with which you encountered it.***

mahātria

4

What is Dinacharya? How does it help in developing self-discipline?

*D*inacharya is a very important Vedic concept. It is derived from a Sanskrit term: *Din* - daily; *Charya* - routine, behaviour, close to. The belief is that what you do on a daily basis will give you far greater results than anything else that is practiced intermittently, however well it may be practiced.

Brushing of teeth is a *dinacharya*; bowel clearance is a *dinacharya*; eating is a *dinacharya* - but these are natural compulsions.

Gossiping or watching TV could also be *dinacharya* for many people – but they are destructive activities.

A fitness regime or yoga every day, daily meditation or introspection, learning something new every day, reading before sleeping, eating together as a family at least one meal a day are all constructive *dinacharyas.*

Embrace a few constructive activities that you will practice on a daily basis... absenteeism under any circumstance is not permitted. If you absent yourself, it is not *dinacharya*.

In other words, *dinacharya* means '365 – 1 = 0' (Read ' – ' as minus). Let us derive inspiration from that. For a start, let the goal be 'positive greater than negative'.

That is, let the days we observe a constructive *dinacharya* be more than the days we miss it.

Let us break 365 days in a year into 52 weeks. In a week of 7 days, can we first challenge ourselves for a '4>3'? That is, what is right will be practiced, at least for 4 days and absenteeism will be restricted to a maximum of 3 days. Then, make it ‘5 > 2', then ‘6 > 1' and eventually achieve as many weeks as possible '7 – 1 = 0'.

The greatest pride is to grow in one's own eyes! And what better way than to achieve, at least for 27 weeks (27 > 25); ‘positive greater than negative’.

Challenge yourself and grow in your own eyes.

Dinacharya will develop self-discipline in you. ●

Embrace a few constructive activities that you will practice on a daily basis... absenteeism under any circumstance is not permitted. If you absent yourself, it is not dinacharya.

mahātria

I have joined an organization recently. I like my job here but there is too much of gossiping that happens amongst colleagues. I feel uncomfortable in the job because of this. What should I do?

Discussion: What is right.

Argument: Who is right.

Gossip: Nothing needs to be right.

The most uncivilised activity of the civilised world is gossiping. Even the most educated and the so-called elite indulge in this uncivilised activity. Gossip is ruthless entertainment. In gossip, the tongue and the intelligence are let loose. In more than one way, gossiping is vulgar indulgence.

In fact, people come together to form associations and clubs, and gossiping is the lifeline for their fellowship. The most dominant preoccupation of these groups is to discuss about those who aren't present. Never trust a gossiper. After you leave, the one who was gossiping with you will gossip about you with others. Every gossiper will gossip about other gossipers and this is the noble truth.

Hypocrites are those who sweet-talk on the face and bad-mouth behind your back. We shamelessly distort the images of people through gossip, without the slightest care about how much it might affect their lives. Millions of lives will be saved from suicide if the gossipers only choose to be of moral support to the emotionally hurt rather than making news out of them.

Gossip is judgment passed out of half knowledge. Every gossiper eventually drinks his own poison. He becomes highly other-people conscious. His mind is curious all the time - "What are others saying about me?" Judge not and ye shall not be judged. The contrary is also true. Judge and ye too will be judged. Gossipers no more live life through their own spectacles, but instead live to satisfy the spectacles of others.

Curiosity and inquisitiveness are the lifelines for human evolution. When this thirst and hunger for knowledge is canalised towards realising the higher realities of life, growth happens. We make a blunder by feeding this very thirst and hunger for knowledge with gossip. Aristotle, Freud, JK and us - the quest to know is the same. If they had been gossipers, they would have been among us. If we can stop gossiping, we can be among them.

What does a lion have to do among the cats? The next time the gang around you begins to gossip, just walk away. Refuse to speak or hear about those who are not present, especially when what is discussed is judgmental, negative and insensitive. Let our rapture not come at the cost of rupturing the hearts of other people.

Small minds discuss people. Average minds discuss events. Great minds discuss ideas. ●

Curiosity and inquisitiveness are the lifelines for human evolution. When this thirst and hunger for knowledge is canalised towards realising the higher realities of life, growth happens.

mahātria

6

I have been unsuccessful in doing away with jealousy and negative thoughts towards people. How can I achieve purity of thoughts?

An emerging field in medicine is psycho-neuro-immunology. Ever since cancer treatments began to successfully use 'visioning' to encourage patients to mentally fight their cancer, the medical community's interest in positive thoughts and feelings for health has grown. When we are immersed in positivity, our immune system, which is physically linked to the Sympathetic Nervous System (SNS), generates a shower of supportive hormones and chemicals that promote health. The converse too is true when we are down with negative thoughts and emotions. Having prolonged negativity generates showers of inhibitive hormones and chemicals into the system, slowing it down and impairing our functioning and our health. So, you suffer from your own negativity or enjoy your own positivity.

Your negative emotions give you nothing in life, but actually takes away a part of your life. This sustained awareness will eventually become an antidote to your negative emotions. Understand the futility of negative emotions and just let it go.

When someone has something that you don't have or is able to produce results that you are not able to produce, and you are UNABLE TO ACCEPT that - the resultant emotion is JEALOUSY. When someone has something that you don't have or is able to produce results that you are not able to produce, and you are ABLE TO ACCEPT that - the resultant emotion is INSPIRATION.

By being jealous, you are telling your subconscious, "I have a lack." By being jealous, you are telling your subconscious, "I am less." On the other hand, by being inspired, you are telling your subconscious, "What's mine will remain mine, and I don't have to feel insecure about it. What won't be mine, will never be mine, and I don't have to be desperate for it. More importantly, what one man can achieve is proof enough that every man can achieve it, and I too can achieve it."

Jealousy is just a sense of perceived lack but because 'like begets like', your subconscious will, in reality, create that lack in your life and make you feel less about yourself. Instead, get inspired and let your subconscious draw 'more' of everything into your life.

Fighting your negative emotions is no solution. What you resist will persist. Become aware of it; become aware of the negative implications of the same on your life; become aware that negativity gives you nothing in life; become aware that it takes away something from your life. As light would dispel darkness, awareness is the only way to outgrow negativity. ●

Your negative emotions
give you nothing in life,
but actually,
takes away a part of your life.
This sustained awareness
will eventually
become an antidote to your
negative emotions.

mahātria

7

I am unable to control my thoughts.
All the time my mind is cluttered with thoughts.
I am unable to focus.
What should I do?

Psychologists have estimated that on an average we have as many as 60,000 thoughts per day. More importantly, 95-98% of these 60,000 thoughts we process are repeated daily. Each of these thoughts, at the physical brain level, is releasing a shower of chemicals. Neuro-scientists estimate that the human brain contains 100 billion neurons. Each neuron has about 1,000 connections. Each connection fires, on an average, 200 times per second resulting in 20,000 trillion calculations per second! And all this consumes loads of life energy. Even if we can reduce the number of thoughts by a small percentage, it can have a huge bearing on our life. Practicing silence for a few minutes every day gives you the power of that conserved energy.

When we succeed in reducing the quantity of thoughts, we will start observing a remarkable improvement in the quality of thoughts. How? When we reduce the number of thoughts, then the thought congestion comes down and we will be able to hold every thought a little longer. The longer we can hold on to a thought, the more potent the thought becomes. Every thought has creative power and the longer we hold a thought, the more powerful it becomes. With every thought, we send out the essence of ourselves, which mingles with other essences and creates and re-creates our physical environment. In that sense, our life is not our master, but our child. Practicing silence for a few minutes every day gives you the power to create your chosen environment.

Silence is basically vibrations with the highest frequency. The fan blades appear almost extinct when they rotate at great speed. So, when the strings vibrate at their highest frequency, they almost seem like nothing, which is silence. However, it is from these highest vibrations all the relatively lower vibrations originate. Hence, the spiritual expression, everything comes from nothing. Everything is born out of silence. Anything can be created from that state of silence. There is so much scientific truth to the expression, "When a thought is released from the seat of silence, a mere wish becomes a command to the universe." After all, isn't the smallest of particles enough to cause endless ripples in the biggest still-water lake?

Bible says, "Be still, and know that I am God."

Vibrations are transferred only in a state of non-doing. That's the significance of your sitting in the seat of meditation. By sitting in a state of non-doing, either in a space of high vibrations or in the presence of a person of high vibrations, those vibrations will be transferred unto you. That's why you are asked not to speak in the presence of spiritually evolved people, for it isn't time for doing, but it is time for non-doing.

The power of non-doing is that it enables you to tune in and inherit the higher vibrations, and in the presence of higher vibrations, all things are possible. Everything is possible.

That's why Franz Kafka says, "You do not need to leave your room. Remain sitting at your table and listen. Do not even listen, simply wait, be quiet, still and solitary. The world will freely offer itself to you to be unmasked, it has no choice, it will roll in ecstasy at your feet."

Make sitting in the seat of meditation your *dinacharya*. ●

How to get my thinking right?

Ask right now, "Why is this a bad day?" and your intelligence will manage to give you enough reasons. Ask the same intelligence again, "Why is this a good day?" and it will manage to pop answers to this too. You can be your own devil's advocate, thinking for and thinking against the same aspect of life. It is just a question of the direction your thinking provides to your intelligence. Think troubles and your intelligence will give you a stock of your troubles. Think solutions and your intelligence becomes a solution provider.

First make the prejudiced pre-decision, "This person is wrong." After that start thinking where he is wrong, and your intelligence will substantiate your decision that the person is wrong in enough and more ways. The contrary too is true. Sometimes you are so prejudiced towards a person that you believe, "He can never be wrong. He is always right." Now, your intelligence will supply you with enough details to validate your belief. So, right and wrong, is mostly a pre-judgement, and your intelligence only works in the direction of validating that judgement.

Get the direction of your intelligence right by getting your thinking right. And, get your thinking right, by thinking more and more in 'SO', instead of 'BUT'.

I want to exercise, but... I want to start my own business, but... I really want to give quality time to my family, but...

I definitely want to quit smoking, but... 'But' is negation. You are expressing a desire and in the same breath, with a 'But', you are explaining why you are not able to or cannot do it. This thought pattern will take you nowhere.

I want to exercise, so... I want to start my own business, so... I want quality time with my family, so... I have decided to quit smoking, so... 'So' is progression. You are expressing a desire and with the same heartbeat, with a 'So', you are directing your intelligence to find ways to make it happen.

It is startling even to think how much you can accomplish, if you stop thinking 'Why it cannot be done', and instead start thinking 'How it can be done', even if it means that you don't have the answers yet. It is far better to wait without an answer in the right direction than to find an answer in the wrong direction.

To get your life right you have to get the direction of your intelligence right.

It is not your intelligence, but it is the direction of your intelligence that determines the pace of your progress. People who succeed do not necessarily have a higher intelligence, but have a better direction to their intelligence. ●

“

Get your thinking right, by thinking more and more in 'SO', instead of 'BUT'.

mahātria

9

When should I use my intelligence and when should I turn towards my heart? Last time my quick decision after an emotional outburst ruined me.

You analyse with your intelligence. And, you wonder through your emotions. To facilitate wondering, humans have been designed in such a way that when their emotions take over, their intelligence takes a backseat. If you know too much about astronomy, you wouldn't say, "Twinkle twinkle little star, how I wonder what you are?" You would only say, "Twinkle twinkle little star, I know so much about what you are?" If you know too much about botany, you will not wonder at a huge banyan tree and exclaim, "Wow!" You would only say, it is Ficus Benghalensis. That's why, when you are completely consumed by your intelligence, you cannot be emotional. That's why people who are too contemplative and analytical of a situation, rarely get emotionally involved with the situation.

The converse too is true and that's the cause of most human predicament. When you are in the sway of emotions, intelligence doesn't work. And, to make good decisions, intelligence is required. Obviously, decisions made in the sway of emotions turn out to be regrettable decisions.

If you had waited for another week, you might not have resigned. But you were so upset, so upset, so upset, your emotions clouded your intelligence. May be your boss was wrong, but resignation wasn't the only way to resolve the issue. If only you had waited for your emotions to settle down you would not have sacked your best employee. May be your employee did err, but termination wasn't the only way to resolve the issue. But your emotions got the better of you.

From physical abuse to verbal admonishment to breaking things to hitting yourself - every senseless act is an act performed when the senses are not working. You were too emotional to be intelligent. Suicide itself is a decision taken in the sway of emotions. If only they had passed that transition they would have lived on. If only there was anyone to absorb their emotions during that transition they would have never contemplated suicide.

If only Ravana, who became emotional on hearing his sister's side of the story, had waited for his emotions to settle... If only Sita, who became emotional on hearing the demon Maricha's shouts in a voice that sounded like Rama's, had waited for her emotions to settle... If only Lakshmana had stayed put with Sita till Rama returned, instead of becoming emotional and yielding to Sita's emotional tantrums... If only Rama, who became emotional on hearing a washerman's comments about his wife's chastity, had waited for his emotions to settle... Ramayana would not have been an epic of sorrow.

Actions performed and decisions taken in the sway of emotions will make your life an epic of sorrow. Remember, in the sway of emotions intelligence does not work. So, whenever you find yourself, the other, or the atmosphere emotional... abstain from action, abstain from decision-making and wait a little longer for your emotions to settle.

"Do today what you have to do tomorrow! Do now what you have to do today!" says Kabir.

When you are emotional, reverse what Kabir said. When emotional, it is better to procrastinate! When emotional, what must be done now, do later; what must be done today, do it tomorrow. What's the hurry? There is still a lifetime ahead...

Decide through your mind and relate with your heart. ●

10

What is morally-right character?

Animals have no moral issues as their discrimination is purely born out of their instincts. When it comes to killing for food, or mating, or protecting their younger ones, there are no moral issues in the animal kingdom. Similarly, even we, humans, as children, never understood the concept of good and bad. Our experiences parent us. All of us are bound by our instincts, which are to avoid pain and embrace pleasure. A human being is no different from an animal in this aspect. However, a human being is a thinking animal and a thinking animal is very dangerous.

So, the wise individuals who walked this planet before you and me, to ensure that humans direct their thoughts toward creative endeavours and not towards destruction, established a framework of right and wrong. They expected individuals to adhere to this framework, which we refer to as morality. During the Stone Age, a person could overpower you, and claim your spouse as their own, but in a civilized society, such behavior is considered morally unacceptable. However, the fact remains, though people are expected to uphold moral standards, they have not completely transcended their inherent instincts. People are still enticed by the allure of others' possession. Within every individual, there exists a component that reflects their animalistic nature. A perpetual conflict exists between the animal within and the human being within, a war between the instincts and the conscience.

The irony is, instincts have been shaped by individuals' own experiences, whereas their conscience has only been borrowed and inherited from others. Any day, experiential knowledge is more potent and hence, more often than not, the animal within triumphs over the individual. This split between instincts – the sense of pain and pleasure and conscience – the sense of right and wrong - is what we call character loss. Sin is defined as this split between one's instincts and their conscience. That is why eating non-vegetarian food isn't a character loss for one religion's follower as their religion and personal constitution doesn't consider it wrong; but the same act would be considered a loss in character, if you are from the Jain community. If there is a split, it is a sin. It is called a sin because the individual now is like a cart that is being pulled in two different directions.

A person of character is someone who lives without a split. They have nothing to hide. They abstain from actions that must be hidden from others. They are not someone who think, "Will I be caught or not?" They are someone who think, "Is it right or wrong?".

A life beyond a split is a lifelong quest. It isn't something that man can believe he has arrived at... he keeps arriving... it takes just a moment to slip but a lifetime of resolve to hold on. You have to keep holding on. •

Sin is defined as this split between one's instincts and their conscience.

mahātria

Is there any correlation between my sleeping hours and my productivity during waking hours?

Although it's a common belief that 8 hours of sleep is required for optimal health, a six-year study of more than one million adults in the age group of 30 to 102 has shown that people who get only 6 to 7 hours of sleep a night have a lower death rate. Individuals who sleep 8 hours or more, or less than 4 hours a night, were shown to have a significantly increased death rate compared to those who averaged 6 to 7 hours.

Researchers from the University of California, San Diego (UCSD) School of Medicine and the American Cancer Society collaborated on the study, which appeared in the February 15, 2002 issue of the Archives of General Psychiatry, a journal of the American Medical Association. Individuals who average 6.5 hours of sleep a night, can be reassured that this is a safe amount of sleep. From a health standpoint, there is no reason to sleep longer.

Inside the womb we kept sleeping and again inside the tomb we will keep sleeping. In between these two terminal events we have this life to live and here too, why should we spend it oversleeping?

A human being's lifespan is the time between birth and death. The time of birth was not in our control and the time of death will not be in our control. Thus we cannot control our lifespan. So the equation is, 'Lifespan' minus 'Sleeping Hours' is equal to the 'Waking Hours', with which we experience life. Just by cutting down our sleep by 2 hours per day we can increase our waking hours for an additional 30 days in a year. This means, when the world lives 12 months by sleeping 8 hours a day, in the same period the one who sleeps for only 6 hours will live 13 months.

Three changes have to be achieved to cut down on sleep.

Firstly, improve the quality of your sleep - 6 hours of deep sleep is far better than 10 hours of disturbed sleep.

Secondly, conquer the gap between 'Waking up' and 'Getting up'. We wake up and then get up. However, after waking up we let the body prevail over the mind and we go back to sleep for few more minutes. The lower has prevailed over the higher. If only the mind could take charge over the body in that gap, we would have gained a psychological victory. By not conquering the gap between waking up and getting up, we start the day on a defeat. The very first experience of the day is a negative one - the lower prevailed over the higher. If we cannot even gain control over the body, how are we going to gain control over our life? Conquer the gap and begin the day on a winning note. Begin the day by shaking yourself out of slumber. In the gap between 'Waking up' and 'Getting up', no more hear the habitual "Sleep... sleep." Instead hear the awakening, "Awaken... Awaken."

Finally, have a purpose for the day. People are lazy because they have nothing to look forward to in the day. People become lazy when they pursue impotent goals. Even the laziest will jump out of the bed when he has something to look forward to. To pick up a loved one from the railway station or to drop a friend at the airport or to watch the early morning telecast of a cricket match or when you have to do work that excites you... getting up early becomes a self-motivated affair. Responsible women of the house wake up early, every single day because they have responsibilities they look forward to. Define a driving purpose for the morning and the day, and you may not even need an external clock to wake you up. The awakening call will come from the within.

Sleep will enable you to dream, but you must wake up to achieve them. Wake up. ●

12

I have been a smoker for about a decade now. I have attempted to drop this habit many times. Why am I not able to succeed in quitting any habit including lethargy?

Pain and Pleasure are the two fundamental navigators of human behaviour. The natural inclination is to embrace everything that is pleasurable and avoid everything that is painful.

Why do smokers continue to smoke in spite of all the advices from their well-wishers to give it up? It is because smoking to them, is pleasure and giving it up is pain. Even if they understand the lectures given by others, the pleasure they get out of smoking will continue to draw them into the habit. In the later years of their life when after an open-heart surgery the doctor warns them, "If you continue to smoke, you will hit the grave soon", the same person now gives it up. Why?

It is because, between pain and pleasurable the choice is always pleasure, but between less pain and more pain the choice is always less pain. Now the choice is between the lesser pain of giving up smoking and the greater pain of death, they quit smoking.

As long as pleasure is associated with any habit; that habit cannot be dropped. If a habit has to be dropped, then enormous pain has to be associated with it. We also need to attach enormous pleasure to life without that habit.

Change can come only by reprogramming.

With every experience since birth, we have been strengthening our conditioning. As we begin to look at our own behavior with great maturity, we realise that a lot of aspects in us and about us, has to undergo drastic changes. We desire to change, but struggle to bring about these changes in us. Wanting to change and not able to change breeds a feeling of incompetence in us.

After listening to a lecture or reading a book, we get inspired to change. However the frustration continues for we are only able to change at the intention level and are not able to implement it in action. When sleeping and lethargy is pleasure and jogging is pain, a mere desire will not bring about a change in us. The inner programming of pain and pleasure has to be reprogrammed.

When we realise that excess sleeping is going to rust our biological system and affect our biological clock, when we realise that excess sleeping steals away more than one third of our life we begin to associate pain to sleep.

When we also realise that jogging and exercise burns away the unwanted fat and cholesterol in us, leading to health and fitness, we start associating pleasure to exercises. This reversal of pain and pleasure is called reprogramming by which we will be drawn towards exercises and away from excess sleeping.

Just reading this answer will not create reprogramming in you. Having understood the concept, you must take time off and play this reprogramming in your mind several times. Whether it is swapping TV time with studies or to transcend your senses, reprogramming is required to create a lasting change.

In whichever aspect of life you want to change, identify with what have you associated pleasure and what have you associated pain with. Then take time to reprogram pain and pleasure and play this reprogramming in your mind several times till it brings about a lasting change in your conditioning. Desire will not change you, reprogramming alone will.

You can become the human being you wish to be.

13

How to manage my time?

There are too many concepts on time management... too much literature... too many tools and organisers... let us do a KIS - Keep It Simple. All our activities can be simply classified as: Important, Personal Urgency, Other's Urgency and Insignificant.

Important - it is the zone of discipline. It is those aspects of our life where the seeds of today will become the trees of tomorrow. They don't act on us; it's we who need the discipline to act on them. Discipline is the ability to do things out of free will much before they become a compulsion. Personal urgency - it is the zone of demand. Things that fall under personal urgency always get done, for these activities have their own ways of demanding that time out of you. Others' urgency - it is the zone of delusion. It gives you a sense of preoccupation. They lead you to believe that activities are accomplishments. Insignificant - it is the zone of drain. These activities drain you of your energy and time, but the effects of these activities are completely inconsequential to your growth and progress.

An often cited metaphor explains this clearly. Put some fist-sized rocks into an empty bucket till it is filled to the brim. Into the bucket that appears to be full, you will still be able to add a lot of pebbles, for they will find gaps between the fist-sized rocks. Then, you can add sand and follow it up with water. However, if you first fill an empty bucket with water, then nothing else can be added. It is all about order. It is all about first things first.

Let things which matter most not be at the mercy of things which matter least, just because they are convenient. Whatever is important should first get our time and attention. So, let us first discipline ourselves to incorporate what is important into our lifestyle. Let the fist-sized rocks go in first and take their time. We will then give in to the demands of our personal urgency on a daily basis. Let the pebbles go in next. Let the delusion of others' urgency and the drain of the insignificant - the sand and the water - take whatever is left.

Life isn't about time management, but self-management. It isn't about organising time, but organising ourselves. All of us will realise this in the end, but why wait till the end... why not realise it in the beginning... why not now? Let us not count the days; let us make the days count.

Discipline is the ability to do things out of free will, much before they become a compulsion.

mahātria

14

Friends are an integral part of my life. I am aware that I am heavily influenced by them… sometimes in a negative way too! What should I do?

The company of people you keep is a double-edged sword... it has both the power to create you and the power to destroy you. The company of people we surround ourselves with has a tremendous bearing on the way we think, the way we feel, the way we look at other people, the way we look at ourselves, our present and the future we will create. True, there are people who have emerged 'in spite of' their surroundings... we aren't discussing exceptions; the majority of human minds are shaped by their environment... 'because of' their surroundings.

Your today is not simply shaped by your yesterday; your today is in many ways shaped by the people with whom you spent (or invested) your yesterday. Your tomorrow will be shaped by the people you give your today to.

A member of a certain church, who was a regular at service, suddenly stopped going to the church. A few weeks later, the pastor decided to visit him. It was a chilly evening. The pastor found the man alone at home, sitting before a blazing fireplace. The man welcomed the pastor and led him to a big chair near the fireplace and waited. The pastor made himself comfortable but said nothing. After a few minutes, the pastor took the tongs, carefully picked up a brightly glowing ember and placed it on one side of the hearth, all alone. Then he sat back in his chair, saying nothing. The host watched in fascination. The glow of the lone ember slowly diminished, and soon it was cold and dead. Not a single word had been uttered since the initial greeting. Just before the pastor was ready to leave, he picked up the cold, dead ember and placed it back in the middle of the fire. Instantaneously, it began to glow once again with the light and warmth of the burning coals around it. As the pastor reached the door to leave, his host said, "Thank you so much for your visit and especially for the fiery sermon. I shall be back in church next Sunday."

They say an adopted child in due course of time becomes so much like the family into which they are adopted. True... so we become like the company we keep. If we aren't growing at the pace at which we can, and if we aren't living life with the grace and dignity with which we can, then we may have to make a bold decision... whether it is the company we work for, the company of people we relate with or friend's circle as in your case, if it isn't creating us, we will have to shift ourselves to a different place or group where we can grow. A tough decision it is, but a needed one too. What is the point in wasting a seed in a heap of garbage? ●

"

Your tomorrow will be shaped by the people you give your today to.

mahātria

15

I always struggled to concentrate on one task. I often get distracted by many things just like a child. How can I reach that state where I am able to do many tasks at a time?

Without achieving excellence in single task, excellence in multitasking cannot be achieved. Focus is not only your ability to say 'Yes' to the 1, but also the discipline to say 'No' to the other 99 distractions.

Firstly, start using pen and paper. True, we live in a world revolutionised by technology, but nothing can give a direction to thinking and also keep the mind focused like the use of pen and paper. When we write by hand, the neuro-linguistic association is such that, it does not allow our mind to wander.

Secondly, if you want to train a wild elephant, it has to be first tamed. Practicing 'concentration of mind' will progressively tame your mind. Mind control is the only self-control, and once mind is controlled, everything else is controlled. So, every day, hold your mind in concentration on any object of your choice - it could be watching your breathing, regulating your breath, chanting a mantra, staying connected and offering prayers at the altar of your chosen god or just watching a glowing lamp or the waves of the sea. ●

Focus is not only your ability
to say 'Yes' to the 1,
but also the discipline
to say 'No' to
the other 99 distractions.

mahātria